W9-BIP-772

Books by Pär Lagerkvist
published in the United States and Canada

BARABBAS

THE DWARF

THE ETERNAL SMILE AND OTHER STORIES

THE SIBYL

THE DEATH OF AHASUERUS

THE DEATH OF AHASUERUS

Pär Lagerkvist

TRANSLATED FROM THE SWEDISH
BY NAOMI WALFORD
DRAWINGS BY EMIL ANTONUCCI

Random House
New York

Published in New York by Random House, Inc.
Library of Congress Catalog Card Number: 61-12177
Manufactured in the United States of America

THE DEATH OF AHASUERUS

INTO AN INN for pilgrims to the Holy Land there came one evening a man who seemed chased by lightning, for when he flung open the door the whole sky blazed up behind him; rain and wind hurled themselves at him, and it was all he could do to shut the door again. When at last he succeeded, he turned to the dim room, which was lit only by a few reeking oil-lamps, and seemed to be wondering where he was. It was a big, bare room, and the further end of it was so dark that there he could discern nothing at all. But such part of it as he could see was full of people kneeling in the dirty, muddied straw that covered the floor. They looked as if they were praying; a confused murmur came from them, but he could not see their faces, for they were all turned away; they knelt with their backs to him. The air was thick and stuffy; to one coming in from outside it was almost nauseating, and difficult to breathe. What *was* this place?

Not far from the door, seated at clumsy wooden tables, some coarse-faced men were dicing and drinking. A couple of women were there too, hanging round the necks of the men and apparently as drunk as they. One of them looked up bleary-eyed at the stranger who seemed pursued by lightning. No one else took any notice of him.

There was no vacant place except at one of the tables. Here a man was sitting quite alone. He was gazing abstractedly before him, preoccupied with his own thoughts. He was middle-aged, sinewy and lean; his legs were stretched at full length under the table, and a dog lay curled up at his feet. The stranger went over and sat down near him.

The man did not look up or seem to notice that anyone had approached. The stranger showed no awareness of him, either, beyond a sideways glance at his face. It was a rugged, closed face, covered with prickly, reddish stubble, and with a hard-bitten mouth; it allowed of no approach. His long, thin hands, hairy-backed, lay on the table before him, lit by the little flame of the oil-lamp that flickered in the draught from the door, like a small frightened animal in that great bleak room.

The murmur of the worshippers could be heard continuously, mingled with the rolling of dice on the tables and the drunken voices and laughter of the players. Outside the gale boomed, hurling itself against the wall behind the table; rain beat upon that wall and upon a little window above their heads; it rattled against the blind pane.

The stranger again eyed the man beside him. Useless to ask him anything: where they were, what queer place this was so high in the hills.

The dog stirred, turned, and settled down again by the man's feet with a faint whine. The man seemed not to care about it, or perhaps never noticed that it had moved and rubbed against his split, worn shoes.

Suddenly the whole room was lit by a tremendous flash of lightning; the thunder-clap came almost simultaneously and rumbled on long afterwards among the mountains. The stranger looked about him and up at the window that had blazed in the flash, but was now as dim as before. No other person paid any attention to the raging storm that kept them shut up here. Why were there so many? Why were they kneeling here in the straw?

From one of the tables where the drunken men sat a woman rose and came unsteadily towards them. She stopped and looked for a moment at the man with the dog, then sat down opposite him. For a long time she said nothing; she merely looked at him with a wry, mocking smile. Her mouth went awry when she smiled. She was evidently drunk, and did not trouble to hide it. Her hair was disordered, and lay thick and dark red above the ravaged face which had once been very beautiful—so beautiful that it was almost so even now. Even her mocking mouth was beautiful, large and full; a mouth that drew men to itself.

"Why aren't you drinking?" she said at last, in an unexpectedly deep voice.

When he made no answer she shrugged one shoulder contemptuously.

"I'm drinking. Do you mind? Do you mind my drinking? Tell me!"

"Why should I?" The man turned, looking at her for the first time.

"No, why should you? After all, it was you who taught me."

She turned to the other man at the table, to the queer stranger who had been chased in by lightning.

"It was he who taught me to drink, you see. He taught me everything. Taught me from the beginning—that's why I am what I am. It's all his doing. He's succeeded, don't you think? He should be pleased with himself. He started by raping me—he taught me that. And then everything else. He began with the most important thing. Isn't that true? Isn't it? You weren't so holy in those days: you weren't exactly a pious pilgrim. You didn't behave much like a man bound for Jerusalem—or if you were, you were setting about it a funny way.

"He's going to Jerusalem, you see. No, you don't

see, because he doesn't look like that—he doesn't look like a pilgrim—but that's where he's going. To the holy land. If he escapes the gallows, that is."

The stranger looked at her in wonder, then at the man and then at the people who were praying.

"Funny place this, don't you think? Pilgrims and rogues, rascals and saints all mixed up together. It's not easy to tell them apart, I may say; for some fellow praying there may be a bigger scoundrel than any of us; he may be one of us, in fact—it's quite possible—and may have robbed some simple-minded brother kneeling beside him. One never knows. And why not? He has to live too. Everyone must live; though why it should be so necessary who knows? And here everyone lives on pilgrims: on all these crazy folk who are desperate to get to something they call the Holy Land. Why they call it that I don't know, but I suppose one must call it something. And they carry all their belongings with them: their rings and bracelets and silver spoons and cups. Their ducats are sewn into their clothes, which makes them troublesome to get at. These folk look poor, but you may be sure they're not—and a good thing too, or what would become of the rest of us? Some are so rich you wouldn't believe. But those aren't here, of course, in this filthy straw; no, they sleep in the upper rooms of the house—grand, gentlemen's rooms. They have servants to wait on them from morning till night, and coachmen and all; for they travel in their own carriages to their saviour's* sepulchre, and live as they're accustomed to live, all the way there. And why not? There's nothing wrong in that—let them! But what puzzles me is that in this way their servants become pilgrims too; they reach the holy sepulchre too, just like the gentry. What's one to say to that? Surely they oughtn't to count as pilgrims? No, I won't believe it.

"But one of them, you know, one of them's so grand that he has a whole string of carriages. I don't even know how many. He's a nobleman with such a fine name that nobody can even pronounce it, and he's brought more servants with him than you can imagine, though he's quite alone. What do you make of that? Valets and lacqueys run round him wherever he goes, and they guess what he wants

* Publisher's note—Throughout this book the author's use of capital letters in words referring to Christ or deity reflects the degree of religious belief of the characters.

before he even opens his mouth. You never saw such waiting-on as he gets. They say he doesn't even wipe his own bottom, and it must be true because that's what he looks like. And in one of the carriages he has a money-chest so heavy you can hardly move it, they say. But if it's still with him when he gets to Jerusalem is another matter. He'd surely do better to lose it, seeing how hard it is for a rich man to get through the eye of a needle. According to Scripture. Because that's Scripture all right, isn't it? Eh?"

The murmur of prayer ceased, and when the stranger turned he saw that the people were settling themselves for the night, rolling their cloaks for pillows and lying down to rest in the dirty straw. They lay fully-dressed, as if prepared to leave at any moment and continue their journey.

He tried to see their faces; he much wanted to see them, and many of the people were now standing with their faces towards him. Most of them wore no particular expression, but others were lit with something that filled him with wonder and troubled him. It was something that he had encountered in people before, occasionally, and he had always found it baffling.

The woman too sat looking at them, and for a time she said nothing more.

"Some are honest and pure-hearted, no doubt," she continued, presently, in a different tone. "Some may even be saints of a kind, and will know eternal bliss. It's always possible. Though one can never tell . . .

"Imagine it: there's a girl who lies with them—with any pilgrim who wants her—so as to earn money for her own pilgrimage; all her expenses. Could you have imagined such a thing? I've talked to her myself; I asked her about it, and she told me it was true. She said it was the only way for her to reach the Saviour's sepulchre, which she so longs to visit—which she *must* visit, for her soul's happiness. That's all that means anything to her, she says; nothing that she has to go through to attain it matters at all, for she holds her body of no account: she sacrifices it willingly, that her soul may find peace at the journey's end. Did you ever hear of anything so queer? She gets no pleasure from it, she told me, when I joked about it a bit; just now and again, perhaps; and she hoped this might be forgiven her, for she was sinning not for her own delight, but in order to bend her knee at her Saviour's tomb. She had never lived like this before; she'd never had anything to do with men. You don't believe this, either of you—but I do; I know it must be true. For she's like that; you can see she's not the kind to want to lead that kind of life. She's forced to, for the sake of accomplishing her pilgrimage. And she must earn enough for the sea-passage too; for the ship to the Holy Land. That costs a great deal, and the money must be found somehow. But she says she cares nothing about the disgrace; she doesn't mind what they do with 'this body, this quite worthless body . . .' That's how she talks. Peculiar. You can't imagine how queer it is to listen to her . . . I like her, I think a lot of her . . . I've had many talks with her, today and yesterday, and each time it seems to me queer . . . 'this worthless body . . . this quite worthless body . . .' "

Suddenly she gave a sob and burst into violent weeping. Her shoulders shook, and she held her hands to her florid face as if to hide it.

But after a while she raised it again and looked tearfully but resentfully at the man with the dog.

"You, now! Where did *you* get the money for your passage? How did you earn it, tell me that! Can you tell me? Or shall I? In no honest way, that's certain. Not like her. She's honest. Her saviour is sure to think her honest, and receive her when she comes, and give her peace. But you're dishonest—you know you are—and so am I. But I haven't always been so; once I was quite different from what you've turned me into, you and your . . . you and your . . ."

She shook her fist at him, but then dropped it again as if sensing the futility of it all—as if it weren't worth quarrelling about. She sat and looked at him with something of the indifference of despair in her tipsy eyes.

Her mouth twisted again in its crooked smile; she shrugged one shoulder as if to express what she thought of him, and shoved at the dog under the table with her foot.

"What sort of a mangy old cur is that you're trailing round with you? Can't you even keep a proper dog?"

"Don't touch him!" said the man, with unexpected heat.

"I shall if I want to. As much as I like. I detest mangy old . . ."

She kicked it, and the dog yelped.

The man sprang up to his full height, lanky and sinewy, with real menace in his look.

"Don't you dare touch him, I tell you! D'you hear?"

He seemed in such a passion that she was amazed, bewildered.

"What's the matter with you? What's got into you? That pitiful cur . . ."

She was at a loss to understand him.

The man had sat down again, but his eyes were still on her, and they were dangerous eyes, which looked as if they might easily turn savage, though why just at this moment there was no telling. The stranger who was seeing these two for the first time wondered at them greatly.

There was silence for a while. Neither of them spoke.

"Don't take so much notice of my chatter, Tobias; you know I don't mean half of it," she said then. "At least we can be friends, can't we? I was miserable when you went off like that without a word. Why did you? Did you think I'd hang round your neck? How could you fancy such a thing! But where did you get to? And where have you been all the time? Well, well, you needn't tell me; it's none of my business. I've no right to interfere —how should I have?"

The dog under the table uttered a plaintive little whine. She peered down and looked at it as well as she could in the half-dark.

"It's a funny-looking dog, though. I've never seen such an ugly brute. Where did you get it? Don't you know what a dog ought to look like? I thought you did."

The man made no answer, but continued to stare her straight in the face.

"Remember my dog, do you? Do you? Oh, when I think of him! Black, glossy coat, shining flanks and a cold white muzzle, and this tongue always hanging a long way out—that was a real dog, a hunting dog!

"He never liked you, do you remember? Not surprising really that he flew at you—he was so fond of me. Oh, how well I remember him, although it's so long ago. I can never forgive you for taking my dog away from me—never."

"*I* took him from you?"

"Yes, it was your doing—your fault that I had to get rid of him, stab him to death. If only I'd done it at once instead of letting him come with us when we set off . . . How could I bear to see him among all those other curs in the baggage-train: horrible, verminous creatures; how could he have gone on living there? He, a dog that was used to freedom, to life in the woods—a hunting dog! And when I saw him beginning to look like the rest, with piteous, cowardly, watery eyes . . . To me there's nothing worse than miserable, cringing dogs—dogs to be pitied!

"I don't want to think about that; I want to think of how it used to be. Do you remember when we lived there in the forest together, the dog and you and I . . . lived by hunting . . . when I taught you how to hunt, to live as one ought to live . . . how to bring down a running deer . . .

"Do you remember that funny name you found for me: Diana? It's not a name at all—no one's called that; you just made it up. And I didn't like it, so you had to stop. But those were lovely days, weren't they? Weren't they? Until you had to go back so as not to be separated from your league, or whatever you called it—everything you men invent has some silly name; it's all so stupid and sounds so silly. Diana . . . though that's not a name and no one can be called that. But we had good times, didn't we? Don't you think so—didn't you think so? Ah, there aren't many days to be happy in, not very many. What do you say, Tobias? Are there?"

He didn't answer.

She stroked the worn wood of the table with her hand, where his hand also rested. The stranger looked at both their hands there on the table.

No one said anything more.

From the drunken party came a rough, raucous voice:

"Aren't you coming? What are you sitting there for? Aren't we ever to finish the game?"

The woman made a grimace of disgust and rose unsteadily, leaning a little on the table.

"That's the rabble I'm with. That's where I belong. It doesn't matter . . . nothing matters . . ."

She looked at him for a moment with her dark, over-bright eyes, and then went back to the place where she belonged.

"She's mad," the man muttered to himself when she had gone. But he was evidently deeply agitated.

"Was anything of what she said true?"

The man threw a glance at the questioning stranger, as if wondering what it had to do with him. But although he was long in answering, it was plain that he needed to talk, to communicate with someone.

"True! Of course it's true—in a way. Though not all of it. Or at least not in that way."

"In what way then?"

"Well. We did live together, as she said, in the forest; that's true. And it's true that those were really wonderful days.

"I'd left the others and was roving on my own . . . yes, I was a soldier; there was war, of course, there always was . . . I was really a poor young scholar, but how could anyone go on with that? It was impossible—everything was impossible; the whole town had gone, for that matter, except for smoking heaps of ruins. So one had to become something else—a bandit or a soldier, whichever it might be; there was little to choose between them. I turned soldier. And as we were stalking through those great woods, near to where we had pitched camp—soldiers are always nervous of woods, so a few of us were out to make sure that there was no danger in them—well, as we were doing that I got separated from the others and roamed off on my own.

"At last I came to a glade among the trees where the grass was beautiful and thick, and in the middle was a spring. And by that spring was a woman. At first I wasn't really sure that it was a woman, but it was, and not a man, though she almost looked like one. She was bending over an animal, cutting it up, and beside her a dog was busily devouring some of the entrails that she had tossed to it. When she heard my footsteps she sprang up like lightning with the bloody knife in her hand, ready to defend herself; the dog rushed at me barking furiously, and set upon me, so that I was hard put to it to hold it off.

"But I took it all calmly; I walked over and

wrenched the knife from her hand just as she raised her arm, and asked her rather reproachfully whether she meant to take my life. A superfluous question, for that was clearly what she had intended. Then I said that I only wanted to drink at the spring, and might I not do so? As she didn't answer I lay down at the brink, but saw that there was blood in the water, because she had been rinsing her dismembered quarry in it. It made me pause a little, and I said something about there being blood in the water. She stood looking scornfully down at me, and I noticed then that her mouth went a little crooked when she smiled, but that was her only fault; she was almost as beautiful as a woman can be. And she wore no more than a piece of deer-skin, so I could see the shape of her.

"'Are you so frightened of a little blood?' she said, with that mocking smile.

"I made no answer; I just drank.

"And when I had drunk I raped her, and her smile was partly to blame for that, for it would have set any man on fire.

"So what she says is quite true. But there was nothing unusual in my conduct, for we all did the same when we came upon a woman. And this one was such that it would not have been easy to resist her.

"And it's true too that the dog, which had been quieter for a while, now flung itself at me savagely, and bit me all the time till the blood flowed, though I paid no attention to this. She also raged at first and resisted violently; it was almost like wrestling with a man, so strong was she. Yet before it was over we had become friends enough to stop actually fighting; she even condescended to kiss me, although her smile was still a little scornful when she did so.

"That was our beginning. And since then she has often admitted that in fact she too really enjoyed it.

"For my part, of course, I was delighted: so greatly delighted that I stayed with her there in the woods and let the others think I had got lost, as indeed I had. I had never had such a woman before, nor perhaps have many other men. I mean of course as she was then; not afterwards. She wasn't like ordinary women; nothing about her was ordinary. So one felt unsure—and strangely enough she too seemed to feel unsure; one could see that from her tense, challenging manner. One had to keep on one's guard—for she was always on hers. She never quite surrendered, and one never knew where one was with her, not even when one lay with her—not even then did one seem to come really close. She was like a virgin whom no one could utterly possess.

"She couldn't disguise her enjoyment of what was for her a new experience; yet at the same time she seemed timid—almost afraid—and would try to avoid what she so desired for as long as she could. To the very last she fought against it, and especially against complete surrender. Never have I seen a woman look so tormented at the moment of fulfilment. Was this perhaps because her pleasure was in fact keener than others'? Can you tell me why women smile so painfully at the moment when they most delight in being alive?

"So that's how we went on together. Loving her was troublesome and uneasy, but that was probably what made one do it.

"And certainly we were happy. We roamed about the woods and camped whenever and wherever we felt like it. She had no special camping place—at least not then when it was summer. In the winter I suppose she lived in some cave or other. There was game in plenty and she brought it down easily with her simple hunting-gear: the bow and arrows that she had made for herself. When I tried to handle them I had no success; I was used to other, clumsier weapons. Her marksmanship was incredible: nothing escaped once her sharp eyes had spied it. Often I couldn't even see her quarry. It was no wonder I called her Diana; but she had never heard the name before and didn't know what it meant—she knew nothing, for that matter. And it's true that she didn't like it. But that isn't why I stopped calling her so.

"In the evenings we cooked our food over a camp fire, and when she had covered the hot embers with a little earth and moss, as her habit was, we slept beside it.

"How she had come to live alone in the woods like this I don't know. But many strange things happened then—one came upon queer lives and odd ways of living—of surviving—in that time of war and plague and utter confusion, until almost nothing could surprise one any more. And if you think that time is over now—I mean the time when one could experience unbelievable things, incomprehensible, quite inconceivable things, things that the human mind could not grasp—then you're wrong. Really wrong. But that's something else . . . something quite different . . .

"Perhaps all her kin were dead or had vanished through war and plague. Or perhaps she never had any? I don't know. I never found out. When I asked her she would simply shake her head, as if she thought it a quite unnecessary question. She made one feel as if she had never lived in any other way than this.

"When I was obliged to return to the army, to the camp, she came with me. And that she did this must have meant that she cared for me—was bound to me in some way; or perhaps she could no longer do without what I had given her. I can only say that although I wanted her to come I never forced her. That I dragged her with me, as she's often declared, is untrue, and she knows it. She made up her own mind, as she always has. No one can gain any real power over her.

"She left her forest and her hunting life and

joined the camp-followers. What else could she do if we were to go on living together? You can imagine what sort of women those were. She became one of them. Soon afterwards we broke camp and went away to other places, and to new feats of arms and pillage.

"It was not my fault that before very long she became common property to the company. I wanted her to myself, of course, but the others made this impossible. And I'm not sure that she was satisfied with just me any longer, or that she minded being taken by others—by many—and being exploited and prized as she deserved. It's not easy to know exactly, and she altered so much that I no longer understood her. But that I'd never done, nor had anyone else. I was tormented by what was happening to her and thought about it a great deal; and I needn't say that I was more in love with her than ever, now that other men possessed her too.

"For we didn't drift apart and become indifferent to each other because she went with so many men. It wasn't like that. We were attached to each other, and she lay with me too; and there may have been something special in our relationship, and in us when we were together, because we reminded each other of so much in our past, when everything had been different. That was something she could never share with casuals—with all those other men. We were the only ones with memories.

"But it was never again the same as in those days. We could still have joy in one another if we didn't demand too much, and now we no longer needed to be on our guard with one another; there wasn't the same tension between us, and when I loved her she didn't resist, but kissed me and caressed me all the time, from the beginning. But I never called her Diana again.

"The war went on for many years, and during this long time she decayed, as they say, more and more. But no doubt I did too, though in another way. We all do. She lived in the midst of brutality, whoring and drunkenness there in the baggage-train, among those lecherous women whom the army dragged with it until they became so worn out, used up and ill that they straggled behind or were chased away, while in their place others were sucked in on the march through that ravaged, plundered country. She became like the rest, or almost like them; for she could never be altogether like them. Her face altered, its young, firm features slackened and dissolved, her speech grew coarse and shameless, and her once lovely deep voice became rough and hoarse from so much drinking. She began to get as she is now, which meant of course that I felt more and more distaste for her, though I was still bound to her and desired to be so. She must have meant something to me still. To others she was just one of the harlots in the baggage-train, but for me she was something else as well—something that I had once met by a spring in the woods. Sometimes I reflected that her bow and arrows were still lying there in the moss, and that by now, perhaps, the moss had grown over them.

"Then the war came to an end at last—if such a thing as war can end. We soldiers were disbanded —'sent home,' as they called it, although we had no homes and turned bandit instead. A good many of us, anyway. We formed robber gangs and roved about, snatching whatever was left in that devastated, squeezed-out land. I joined one of the gangs; what else was there to do? One has to live somehow. And she stayed with me as before. When it came to the point she always stuck by me; it was almost as if without me she would have felt unsure of herself, somehow; uncertain and lost in this strange alien world, to which—for all her coarse manners—she didn't really belong. It was as if she couldn't do without me: without someone who knew of her past—knew who she really was. As if she must always be near that person.

"So now she became the robbers' harlot. They needed such women, and at times they gave her other work to do—work better suited to a woman than a man. She had the advantage of being both, in a way, and on some occasions she could be used just because of that. The men used to laugh at this quality in her, but knew very well how to exploit it. And they laughed because she seemed to despise them: they wouldn't believe it was true, because she willingly lay with them. But it was true. Of course she despises us men—all of us. Yet at the same time she wants to be like us. She wants to feel like a man or almost like one; it's really *she* who wants to possess *us*.

"She came with us on our various enterprises, which were often strange enough, and was very useful in many of them. And when she says she dislikes this life, which at times can be so exciting, and dislikes this company—this rabble, as she calls it—I just don't believe her. I believe she's really quite content with it all and with these rough characters, although she despises them and is different from them. Certainly she would not wish to leave them and their life.

"But now the two of us grew further and further apart, and I preferred to have nothing more to do with her. This mannish woman with her sneering, crooked mouth and insolent talk and almost always bloodshot eyes was too far away from what I had once known and loved. My feelings for her died, and were followed by disgust and loathing, for her and for all to do with her.

"Disgust and loathing I felt too for the life itself—this life of rough soldiering and banditry—this criminal life that seemed to fill the world, to lay waste the world, expose it to senseless devastation; to shame, misery and despair. The criminal life that I had led so long—I and all these others. Why was I in it, why was I just like all the others? How could I endure it, stoop to it? What sort of life was it?

How could I go on? Thus I questioned myself, and I became more and more revolted by this existence, my own shameless existence, and by myself.

"Yet I stayed on; I didn't break away. I didn't free myself and begin a new life—a life of my own. Not that it would have been easy, of course; how was one to set about it? I just went on in the same way as before, although I scorned to do it.

"I longed for a change; I longed to get away from myself and from all that surrounded me; and although I did nothing about it, my mind was busy. Sometimes there even came into my head something that I must have thought or read long ago, and no longer quite recalled; a memory of something besides this—something quite different—something that I'd forgotten and lost.

"People puzzle themselves so much about what they're to live on—they talk and talk about it. But what is one to live *for?* Can you tell me?

"What's one to live *for?*"

He sat staring before him with his light gaze, and seemed to be far away.

Outside, the storm roared; from the sleeping pilgrims in the darkness came the sound of heavy breathing, and here and there the whisper of one who still prayed. The oil-lamps at the further end had been put out, and there was light now only by the tables.

"Is it really true that you're a pilgrim?" asked the stranger after a time. "How did you come to be that?"

For a long while the man made no answer. Clearly he was shy of talking about this; it was repugnant to him. He sat looking down at the heavy table-top, worn and darkened by long use, and passed his thin hand back and forth along it.

"It wasn't that I left them," he began at last. "I didn't give up the life I was leading. It wasn't like that. I just happened to be out on my own that day, roaming about with no real aim—without any aim at all. It was none of my doing.

"I've always liked wandering about, being alone, at peace. Perhaps that day I felt more need for it than usual—more need to get away from the others; I was weary of this meaningless existence, of the pointlessness of everything. I may have felt it more than ever that day. I didn't notice which way I was going, and so I simply got lost. I didn't know where I was. But I didn't care; I went on as before. I'll get back in time, I thought.

"The region I was walking in was deserted. That I'd already seen, but now I saw how deserted it really was, and in what way. It was no wilderness, but cultivated land; yet the fields lay untended; they could not have been tilled for a very long time, for they were full of saplings and bushes and here and there half-grown trees; the forest had broken into those fields again and won them back. Not a soul was to be seen anywhere, nor any trace of one. It was forsaken.

"It came as no surprise, for many places were in the same state. For years war had rolled its devastation over this land, and was no doubt the cause of its neglect. And perhaps there were no folk left to cultivate it. After the war, plague had spread more swiftly than before, and claimed many more victims than the war itself; whole tracts of country were quite depopulated, and lay abandoned and desolate. But such a waste as this I had never seen. Here reigned a quite peculiar silence and emptiness; a stillness which was awe-inspiring. It was penetrating. It penetrated me, I felt.

"Not a single human dwelling was to be seen. But at a distance were some old trees which seemed to be growing in a hollow, since only their tops were visible. They were not far away, and although the day was far advanced I went forward to see what the place was like. I found that down there, in a long, narrow glen, lay a little hamlet of simple cottages and farmyards, lining a road that ran from end to end of the hollow. I went down to it and along the road.

"The houses were empty and almost all of them doorless. The dark openings led into what had once been the dwellings of men. Nettles and other weeds had begun to grow over the thresholds on to the earth floors. I entered some of the buildings to see if any living creature remained, but of course there was no one. Inside was the same emptiness, except perhaps for some broken, worthless household implement tossed into a corner. Probably the hamlet had been plundered after whatever disaster had befallen it and its inhabitants.

"I own that all these barren, forsaken homes oppressed me, although I was hardened to such sights. It was difficult to account for the desertion, though easy enough to guess that something terrible had happened: some great disaster. Had the people left in terror? In despair? Had it happened suddenly? War, terror, famine, some frightful disease—any human misery might explain what had come about.

"I had walked right along the road without finding the smallest sign of human life. But at the very last house, which stood where the road ended, there was something that struck me and surprised me. It was a very modest house, smaller than the rest, but it had a door. And leading to it was a track through the grass—a very faint one; you couldn't be sure that it was a path at all. If so, it was long since it had been regularly used. I was naturally surprised and curious, so much so that I walked up to the little house.

"The door was shut. When I opened it I found myself in a small room: the only one. One could see at once that it was inhabited, though signs of this were few, and everything in it spoke of extreme poverty. As I looked about I saw a bed along one wall; on it a woman was lying with her face turned upward and her hands clasped on her breast. A dog lay curled up at her feet.

"The dog got up with a whine and looked at me with tired, moist eyes. It was a starved, pitiful little creature with a thin, yellowish coat. When I approached it jumped down from the bed and rubbed itself against my leg, then jumped up again and lay down as before at the woman's feet.

"I bent over her. Then I saw that she was dead.

"Her body, which was utterly emaciated, lay stretched on a little straw and over her were some rags and tatters that failed even to cover her. She seemed of middle age, but was so gaunt that it wasn't easy to be sure. After all the suffering that she must have endured, her face wore an expression of serenity, of solemn stillness. I stood and looked at her, full of wonder, moved by this unexpected encounter with death—by this singular experience—after my walk through the waste lands and the deserted village.

"But the remarkable thing was not my discovery of her, in all her wretchedness, nor her lonely death in this utter desolation. The remarkable thing was . . ."

"Well?" asked the stranger, as the man paused.

"The remarkable thing was . . . that she bore the stigmata."

"The stigmata!" exclaimed the stranger, with a violent start.

"Yes. I saw the marks on her hands at once, and when I uncovered her feet, they were pierced too."

"What are you saying!"

"It's past understanding. But so it was."

"Are you really sure of this?"

"Yes, indeed. I saw it with my own eyes. And I was just as staggered and agitated by it as you—as you seem to be. I was quite unhinged by it, and behaved most oddly, I must confess. How little a persons knows of himself; it's very strange . . ."

"What do you mean?"

"I mean . . . As I was standing there I suddenly fell on my knees beside her . . . *to* her."

"Oh . . ."

"Yes. I don't know why myself."

The stranger sat silent, but his thin hands moved restlessly over each other. Both men were quiet for a time.

"She certainly hadn't been dead long," the man

resumed. "There were many signs of that, and there was not the slightest smell in the room. But that might be because the body was so emaciated. Probably she had lain there a long time without food, having nothing to eat. There was no food of any kind in the house. There was a little ash in the fireplace and a few half-burnt logs, but nothing to show what had happened before her death.

"The daylight was beginning to fade, and you might think I would go away and not care to stay there in the dark with a dead person, whom I didn't know anyway, and had no connection with. But I didn't want to leave her. I didn't want her to lie alone there in the dark, the night after her death; she'd been alone long enough already. Someone should keep vigil, I thought, and watch by the dead. And since I had come here by chance, led by something outside myself, I was surely the one to do it.

"I sat down on a bench by the fireplace, and darkness descended on the room, on the dead woman and myself. On the village too, and the desolate lands where no one now dwelt.

"It was then, during that long night, that I decided to be a pilgrim. When I thought of her fate, of her unspeakable sufferings, and of how she must have lain there yearning for another Golgotha, where the agonies and wounds were not only those of a human being—where amid the pain a miracle occurred, a transfiguration—then it was that I made up my mind to go on pilgrimage to the place where her thoughts must always have been while she herself was suffering. I wanted to do this for her: it was the least that could have been asked of me. I wanted to go on pilgrimage for her sake. Not my own. Well, for my own sake too, of course; that goes without saying . . . but . . . oh, it's complicated, and I don't really understand it . . .

"I was confused about it that night, when I made up my mind—it has grown no clearer since—not yet . . .

"No, I don't really understand it . . .

"But this is something I'm going to carry out—something I must carry out, no matter what happens afterwards. It's a sacred duty. No, not a duty. A sacred promise that I made. Made . . . well, made to myself."

He sat staring in front of him, frowning, evidently troubled by what was stirring in him.

"It was a long night. I thought it would never end. And I had no easy time of it, I must say, because I was thinking so much about what I've just told you: the thing I couldn't understand. And about her too, away there in the darkness—about all human misery, and my own. About the mystery of human destiny.

"It was so quiet that the whole world seemed dead. What sound *could* there have been? There was nothing to disturb the stillness in that utterly deserted world.

"All that happened—somewhere about midnight, I should think—was that a horse came along the road; it must have been a horse. That's what it sounded like. And it was lame. It couldn't put its weight on one leg; one could hear that plainly—more and more plainly as it approached. When the road ended it turned up the path to the dead woman's house, sniffed at it—at the end wall, the window; it went all round the house, and at last sniffed for a long time at the door. It was as if the animal had been in the habit of coming here and doing this. It may have known that one person was left here: one of the people who used to live in this place. After a time it went away, its limping gait sounding from further and further down the road.

"At last dawn began to break, and it came as a relief. When there was real light the dog came down from the bed and again rubbed itself against my leg, whining. Then once more it jumped up and lay down moaning beside the dead woman. This it did several times, as I stood once more looking at her to whom I had bound my fate, and wondering what to do next.

"Or was it she who had bound me to *her* fate? I couldn't tell.

"I knew that the first thing to think of was her burial. I lifted her—she was so light as to seem unreal—and carried her out into that lovely morning; for it was indeed beautiful, with the early sun shining on the grass and on all the trees. Some distance from the house there was a little slope, well-situated in the sunshine, and I carried her there. And having found a spade in the shed next the house I dug a grave for her. And while I was doing this I noticed the lively birdsong all about me. It was strange, for the day before, out in the desolate countryside, I had heard no birdsong at all. Had there been none then, or had I just not noticed it? Now it was morning, and they may have been singing for joy at that. They have their own joy. Why shouldn't they sing?

"When I'd filled in the grave I stood for a while with bent head; and that was her only service. I said no prayer, or anything of that kind, for it's not my way. Then I left, the dog following closely at my heels. It stayed close to me, right at my feet, and it still does.

"Now we've come here to join the pilgrims.

"But I'm not one of them."

With that he ended. Afterwards he sat withdrawn into himself.

The calm breathing of the sleepers came from the darkness; but some who perhaps could find no peace for their souls turned and tossed uneasily.

"No; you may be right there," said the stranger, "when you say you're not one of them. Would you like to be?"

"Perhaps—in a way. But I could never fit in among them."

"Why not?"

"When they kneel there, praying and confessing their sins, I realise that it's not for me. I don't want to do such a thing, however many sins I may have committed. I don't like kneeling. I've never done it."

"To her you did . . ."

"Yes, I know. That's what's so strange, so mystifying. To her I did. Why? And whom was I really kneeling to? I've asked myself that question many times. Can you tell me?"

To this the stranger made no answer. Nor did he show what he thought of the question, but stared at the floor so that the other man should not meet his eyes.

Indeed the man had never yet met his eyes, and had never even thought of doing so. He was far too much preoccupied with his own thoughts to notice the stranger in whom he'd been confiding.

"It's easy to understand whence her wounds came," said the man in a lower voice than before. "And it was perhaps to him . . . to him that I was really kneeling. What do you think? How do you see it?"

"I? What have I to do with it?"

"No. No, of course not. Nothing. I just wondered, though . . . I just wondered what you thought."

"What I think?"

"Yes?"

"I think as you do, of course, that it was to him you were kneeling. But his way of making you do it was a strange one."

"I think so too."

"His way of gaining power over you."

"Power over me?"

"Yes. An unusual way, I must say."

"Power over me!"

"That's surely the point. What else?"

"Power?"

"Yes. Don't you want him to?"

"No. No, I want no one to have power over me. No one. Neither him nor . . ."

"But you're on pilgrimage to his sepulchre."

"I'm doing it for her sake."

"And for yours too, you told me."

"I'd never have thought of such a thing on my own account!"

"No. You wouldn't. That's how it is. And so he led you to the woman with the stigmata, lying there alone in her desolation. It may have been the only way for him to show you his wounds, which otherwise you cared nothing about. But he made you kneel to them and become a pilgrim. He made you leave everything behind you and be one of the many who make pilgrimage to his tomb. And to make sure—to make sure you wouldn't forget your promise, he sent her dog with you . . ."

The man gazed in amazement at the stranger, although until now he had not so much as glanced at him. But in the poor light he could make out little of the man who sat there with his head bowed over his thin hands which he continually clasped and unclasped on his knee.

"How well you must know him!" he said, a little scornfully, a little sceptically; yet it was clear that he was greatly struck by what the other had said.

Receiving no reply he went on:

"For my part I don't know him particularly well. And I can't say that I feel any particular yearning towards his tomb, his Golgotha. I'm doing it for her, as I said; for the woman who longed to be there herself. What *I* long for I don't know. It must often be thus: one doesn't *know*.

"But *she* knew. And she must have liked to think

that someone had such power over her. She *must* have. But I don't."

He stretched out his legs under the table and altered his position. The dog, perhaps a little disturbed by this, also turned and settled itself by his feet in another way. Almost inaudibly, it whined.

"You must know quite a lot about him," he resumed. "Where did you learn it all?"

The stranger ignored this.

"You seem to know how he sets about catching someone and making him kneel—and become a pilgrim. Does he really go to so much trouble for one person? That seems to me pretty queer."

"I think he goes to any amount of trouble over someone he's chosen."

"Chosen?"

"Yes. There he won't let go. Never lets go. Never releases him. It's easy to see you don't know what it's like to be persecuted by god."

"Persecuted!"

"Yes."

"By god? Is that possible?"

The other man was silent. He was silent in a way that made his words even stranger—ever harder to interpret. Yet he must have meant something special by them. For the first time the man reflected that the unknown person beside him might have a destiny of his own, and existed not only to listen to him. For a long time he looked at him—at his slumped figure and the lean hands clasping and unclasping on his knees.

"What power has he over you?" he asked impulsively.

The stranger seemed struck by these words as by a thunderbolt. He straightened up, raised his head, and suddenly the man met his gaze, which was unlike any human look he had seen before: a desolate look which seemed to come from another age, another world. Those eyes were like wells that had been sucked dry long, long ago.

That look was all the answer he received; and for a long time they sat there without exchanging a word. Rain and wind swept about the house; the dull windows flashed now and then, and the thunder rumbled among the heights.

"Did you take shelter here from the storm?" asked the man at last, for the sake of saying something.

The stranger nodded slightly.

"I understand. It was odd that you should have been driven in here—though of course there's no other place in these hills. Only this one, for pilgrims.

"I wouldn't have come here either, if there'd been any choice. Never. And when we go down into inhabited places I don't mean to put up at any pilgrims' inn.

"Where are you bound for?"

"I? I?"

"Yes, you. You're no pilgrim. You're not bound for Golgotha or anywhere else, are you? For none of the holy places?"

"I have no holy places to go to."

"No, but there must be holy places. Don't you think so? I mean . . . for other people?"

"I know nothing about that."

The man sat silent, looking at him.

"And you don't kneel to anything?"

"No."

"Not even to god?"

The other was silent.

"And you don't reproach yourself for it? As I do . . . sometimes?"

"No one in the world need kneel to god."

The man started, and shifted his legs abruptly under the table. The dog, which he must somehow have kicked, made complaint. He bent and looked at it.

"Quiet, you!" he said, shoving at it with his foot. "He does nothing but whine."

The woman whom he had once called Diana came back to their table, even more drunk than before, and sat down opposite the man.

"Those swine—they're all tipsy now. I can't stand them any longer. Even that blackguard who palms off sham amulets and crucifixes on them is drunk: the one who makes out he's a monk—and so he may be, for that matter. I don't know. And that Hubert fellow who never leaves me alone. All of them! The whole gang's drunk—and what good they'll be tomorrow if there's any honest work to be done I don't know. You've got to be sober to do a job properly, haven't you? Miracle-working crucifixes—did you ever hear of such a thing! He cheats them into buying them. And indulgences for as many sins as you like . . . he makes them himself, writes them, I mean. And he can cheat at cards almost as well as I can. What a rabble you've thrown me into; it's all your fault that I've landed among them, isn't it, now? And then you slink off, saying you're going to be a pilgrim—that you've got to go to the Saviour's tomb and the Holy Land —and leave me here among scoundrels and bandits who live by robbing pilgrims, robbing all the others who are bound for the same place. Shame on such creatures— I can't think why I ever wanted to keep company with you. I tell you, even Hubert's a better man than you, for at least he's an honest rogue—a rogue only, not a mixture of rogue and half-saved fraud like you. And he loves me, if you want to know—he really loves me, and I him, though he disgusts me as only a big, fleshy man can disgust a woman. Ugh!

"And who are you?" she said, breaking off suddenly and turning to the other. "Oh, yes, you were sitting here before; I remember you now. How queer you look; you look as if you died long ago. Why didn't you? Not that it's any of my business.

You've got such funny eyes, I mean . . . enough to scare anybody.

"You don't say much, but you may be clever enough, for all that. You look as if you were—with those eyes, and so old as you must be—but it's all the same to me, all the same. Nothing matters —nothing!

"What are you both sitting here giggling for, anyway? Eh? And not even drinking. Where's the sense in just sitting? But here comes old Elizabeth, so the lights will be put out now. Those swine won't be able to drink any longer—look, she's going to tell them so, do you see? Quite right! She keeps law and order in the sty—and if there's not so much order, that's not her fault. Is it now? Can she help what people are like? Eh? Can she help if all kinds of riff-raff gather wherever there are pilgrims? Because they do. Pilgrims attract the scum of the earth. And this house is full to bursting with pilgrims, so that brings more scum, of course. And they themselves are the worst scum of all. Can she help that? I ask you.

"No, Elizabeth's a good sort: there's nothing wrong with her. I think a lot of her.

"I tell you she's the best person I know—the only one who's really what people ought to be. That's how one would like to be oneself, if one could choose. But who can? Who can choose—for himself—how . . ."

She gave a sob and wiped her nose hurriedly.

"What she's done, year after year, here in this house: all the good she's done, treating everyone the same—rich and poor, pilgrim and ordinary sinner—you could never imagine. Even God himself, perhaps, hasn't had time to write it all down in his book—not all of it; there's so much, you see. And she's been here all her life, ever since she was tossed in here wrapped in a rag—tossed in through the door—the door you see over there—by a woman whom they found afterwards frozen to death up in the pass. It was a winter's night—or perhaps autumn. She had to slave and toil at everything until she rose to be housekeeper and manager of the place; and she's been that now for as long as anyone remembers. And what she's seen and lived through here during that time—throughout her long life—with all the different sorts of folk who've passed through the house . . . well, imagine it if you can. What she's witnessed and known! No one has seen as much as she. If you know what I mean by 'much.' Do you?"

An elderly woman who walked heavily and with a slight limp came quietly up to their table and told them it was time to go to rest, and that they must put out all the lamps. Her face was worn and weary as if she had been at work all day and needed rest herself. She was short, and tubby about the hips.

"Have you been drinking too much again?" she said to the woman, looking at her with her grey old eyes and leaning a little on the table as if she needed support.

"Yes, dear mother, I have. Does that sadden you? Why do I always make you sad!"

She stroked the wrinkled hand with its prominent blue veins.

"Oh, no. Little things like that don't sadden me. They're not worth it."

"You're good. So you'll forgive me?"

"I shall have to, I suppose."

"Yes, you forgive everything."

"Oh no, I don't. Don't run away with that idea.

Though most people do. It's just that I leave judgment to someone else. He may be stricter than I am, but then he knows so much more. I don't know enough to judge."

"Oh, you do! You know much more than the Almighty."

"Don't talk like that or I shall get really angry with you!"

"But you do, anyway, let him say what he likes. And judge as much as he likes. I only care about what *you* think; I don't want to have anything to do with him."

"The time will come when you'll have to. But we'll hope he's gentle with you. Perhaps he'll find something in you to like; who knows?"

"I wonder what that could be? But that's his affair."

"Yes, it is."

She straightened herself, and looked gravely and searchingly upon the singular stranger, though without surprise at anything about him. Surely nothing could surprise her.

"Well, children, you must go to bed and put out the light. Tobias, you see to that."

She moved her head a little by way of goodnight, and went back into the darkness as she had come.

When they rose from the table, the woman went up to Tobias, stroked his bearded cheek and said, "You're not angry with me, are you?" And with her lips close to his face she whispered, "If you want anything tonight, you know I'm here."

The man made no answer. He bent and blew out the flame of the little oil-lamp on their table. Then he went, closely followed by the dog. The stranger followed too, and they found two places in the straw, so near the outer door that no one had wanted to lie there. They stretched out side by side in the darkness, the dog curling up at the man's feet. When he stirred, unable to rest, the animal moved too, nestling even closer to him with a piteous little whimper.

But the stranger lay perfectly still, staring up into the darkness.

WHEN THE INN came to life next morning and the pilgrims peered eagerly out through the dim windowpanes, they found that the storm was over at last and that the day promised to be really fine. The joy of this, and of being able to continue their journey, quickly spread among them, and everyone pressed to the windows to look out. Someone opened the big outer door and the sunshine flooded in. People hurried out to make quite sure; yes, it was indeed a radiant morning! Briskly they went in again to make ready for departure. They were to start as soon as they could, and everyone was in a hurry to put his belongings together.

The big room was full of people fastening bundles, gathering their possessions into sacks, or busy in some other way with preparations for the start. Some changed their clothes and put on something suited to walking in, others washed meagerly in a tub of water that had been brought in; women combed out their hair after the night, plaited it hastily as well as they could and pushed it beneath their hoods. Some tended their sore feet for the last time before the day's long wayfaring, rubbing in ointment that they had bought from pedlars, who moved about trying to sell still more of their wares. Other pedlars opened boxes of amulets, rosaries and pictures of saints, hoping to do more business; but no one had time for that now. At the last moment a few rogues tried to win something of value from some simpleton by barter; money-changers with their purses full of counterfeit money offered their services, to supply everyone with the currency of the country for which he was bound. An old man shouted that he had been robbed during the night; he discovered this when wanting to pay for something. But no one troubled about him, no one had time. All was commotion and a running to and fro. But some walked there with pale, gaunt faces and glowing eyes, quite unmoved by their surroundings and murmuring prayers as the rosary slid through their fingers. Sometimes they halted, their eyes closed and lips still, passionately clutching the crucifix. The queer stranger, whom no one noticed or paid the least attention to, looked about him in astonishment, and watched them squeezing in their hands that little image of the man who had once been crucified on Golgotha—squeezing so hard that the cross must have hurt them, and cut deeply into their palms. He turned away, but his thoughts were still occupied by this.

All by herself stood a deaf and dumb woman whom no one knew, or knew anything of, neither whence she came nor why she had joined the pilgrimage. At first they had wondered greatly at her, but now they were used to her and paid her no further attention. She was tall and colourless, with thin, pale hair.

A little bell rang out, calling to prayer. All the people paused in their occupations and knelt; the pedlars too, the money-changers and tricksters of all kinds clasped their hands and whisperingly repeated the prayer that was spoken for them. The only one who remained erect was the stranger, but he stood apart and was unnoticed. As he looked out over the kneeling throng he thought of the man with whom he had talked so long the night before, and wondered whether he was among them. He could not see him, but no doubt he was there.

Now food was to be provided for all these people before they began their strenuous day's journey; it might be long before they had any more to eat. Breakfast was set out on the heavy tables near the door. The rough fellows who had sat at them the evening before had disappeared and were nowhere to be seen; they must have left during the night or very early in the morning. There was not enough room at the tables for everyone; and the meal had to be served in shifts. Even so, not all the pilgrims ate here: only the simpler, poorer folk among them. The rich took their meal elsewhere in the house. Having horses and carriages they were in less of a hurry to leave and had not yet appeared. There was dense crowding round the tables, and some people cuffed and shoved, anxious to get as much food as possible. Others sat as if chained to their seats, and ate long and thoroughly —nor were they sparing of drink—until at length they were thrust aside by others. But most of them were moderate, as befitted pilgrims, and some who were mortifying the flesh hardly touched the food; they looked with distaste at the guzzling folk around them and whispered indignantly to each other. It was long before all had been fed.

Now the leaders of the various parties ordered them to assemble in front of the inn, and everyone streamed out. The light that hit them as they emerged almost dazzled them. The sun had by now risen some way above the eastern hills and flooded that mighty landscape with its still cool rays, filling it with the brightness and purity of a new day, and making everything in it extraordinarily clear—even the most distant things—so that one seemed to be seeing the world for the first time. There was a freshness after the rain, as if the land had been newly-created—as if it had come into existence that very morning and was glad of it. Waters rippled everywhere in little rivulets and brooks which wound glittering down the slopes, or leaked over them in falls, and all the valleys were filled with their song. Yes, it was indeed morning, the morning of creation, of resurrection. They stood enraptured, looking about them, thankful for this miracle which they associated with their pilgrimage, and took as a gift from on high. On the very loftiest mountains snow had fallen—the first since the summer—and white peaks rose to the heavens like a song of praise. Exhilarated, the wayfarers too took up a song—a pilgrims' song, the loveliest they knew—about the heavenly Jerusalem that hung in the sky above the earthly one: the place for which they really longed—to which they were on their way. Fair though the earth was, they yet longed to leave it for the celestial city. Amid the singers stood the tall, deaf and dumb woman, looking about her at that vast, unfamiliar landscape.

The stranger observed them from a little distance, as though secretly: their faces, which as a rule were quite ordinary and inexpressive, like most people's, were now radiant; radiant with something not themselves, not their own, but . . . what? He didn't know. How could he know? But something. And how strange it was that these were the same people who just now had been squabbling over their food, and of whom the drunken woman had said so many disparaging things last night.

And there she stood, a little way from him, and she too was looking at that rapturous throng. She was wan and pale, not at all as she had been the day before, and looked very somber and downcast. She seemed to be seeking someone in the crowd of pilgrims; then she went over and spoke to quite a young woman—could it be the girl who earned money for her pilgrimage by loose living? It must be. Yet she did not look like that at all, and she was by no means beautiful. But the woman who had been called Diana talked eagerly with her, in a muted voice, moved by the approaching separation; she would not let go the other's hand. Did she envy the girl who was to set off in this morning hour towards something new—something which she herself could not desire and for which she cared nothing? Did she envy her that?

The girl herself was calm and composed; puzzled, perhaps, by the other woman's agitation, and embarrassed because she would not release her hand. In her ugly, quite coarse features there was no particular elation; she seemed no more than ordinarily glad to be leaving, to be continuing her pilgrimage; yet in her eyes there may have been a glow which was not to be discerned at such a distance. Many things, even the most significant, depend on the distance from which one beholds them, and he would not deny that there might be something in her which he just did not see.

He too was looking for someone in that company: the men called Tobias, who had told him of his remarkable adventures. It was strange. He was nowhere to be seen. He couldn't be there—he was not there among the crowd, which was now complete. It was most strange. And now the column was ready to start. The leaders walked along it, counting the members of their parties for the last time, and found that all were present. The two women who were too weak to walk had mounted their little donkeys, and the man who had injured his foot had long been seated on his impatiently-fidgeting mule. All were ready. Only Tobias was absent. No one asked after him or thought of awaiting him, for no one knew that he was a pilgrim, and he was not really of their company.

Now old Elizabeth came out of the inn, with her slightly halting gait. She too, no doubt, wanted to see the pilgrims off. How many times must she have done this before: watched them move away on their long journey to that inconceivably far country, of which she had heard so much but would never see? Did she long to do the same and set off like the rest, instead of just looking after this house? Had she ever done it? It was hard to tell. Her furrowed, worn old face betrayed nothing. No change appeared in it when at last the train of pilgrims moved off, and the song of Jerusalem rang out again, even more exultant and jubilant than before. She just followed them with her grey look.

But Diana, with her eyes full of tears, stood watching them and the girl, who never turned but, like all the rest, gazed ahead. He heard her give a sob.

At the head of the procession a big, unpainted wooden cross was carried high above the heads of all. It stood out against the mountain-pass to the south, and when the column came up to a height it showed against the sky itself. The stranger watched it being borne forward through that mighty landscape as if the whole earth belonged to it, followed by all those people—all those who were heading for the little city, the insignificant hillock, where once the cross had stood. He remained alone at last, watching . . .

Would he never be forgotten?

He was thinking of this when afterwards he walked out alone, in the broad part of the valley where the inn lay.

It was indeed strange. So many had been crucified on that Golgotha, that little hill to which all now made pilgrimage. Yes, on the same cross as he—the cross they called his, and worshipped as the holiest thing in the world; on this many others had been tortured, for it was used as long as it was serviceable. Then there were all the other crosses before and after his, and all who suffered on them. But he alone was held to be of any account; the rest were as nothing. They had been forgotten long ago; indeed no one had ever cared about them, or had any idea of why they suffered, whether they were guilty or innocent; nothing. Only he was remembered. They all suffered in the same manner as he did, but their suffering had no purpose in it, and so it was forgotten. Only in his suffering was there meaning. And he knew this. He knew. A meaning for all time, for all men; he must have been filled with it when he went up to his sacrificial death. It would be less difficult to endure what had to be endured if one were filled with the majesty and significance of what was coming to pass. It must help a man greatly in bearing his destiny to know that that destiny is so unprecedented, so vast. It could not be the most difficult thing of all to walk up a hill and let oneself be crucified.

They say that his suffering and death are the greatest events ever to have come to pass in the world, and the most significant. Perhaps; that may be so. But how many there are who must suffer without their suffering having any significance at all!

Such were his thoughts as he walked there in his solitude. He walked with a stoop, and never looked about him. Why should he? But now he did raise his head for a moment; and down in a hollow to his left he saw Tobias walking alongside a stream that ran there. He was pacing up and down on the bare ground beside the water, where there was almost a natural road. Restlessly he wandered up and down, followed closely by the drab-yellow dog. Presumably he had sought this place for the sake of solitude. The stranger wondered whether he ought to leave him in peace, but after some hesitation he went down the scrub-covered slope to meet him.

When the man first caught sight of him he seemed on the point of running away. Yet he did not, but merely turned, feigning ignorance of anyone's approach. The stranger came down on to the bare ground and walked towards him.

Although the man was turned away it was clear that he was agitated, and the stranger's approach seemed not to calm him; rather the reverse. But the stranger himself was not altogether calm, for he suspected that he might be the occasion of the other man's trouble, or partly to blame for it.

"Why didn't you go with the pilgrims?" he asked.

Tobias turned round abruptly and looked at him hard.

"Why should I? I'm no pilgrim, and never will be."

The stranger looked down, avoiding his eyes; yet he had seen them. And that thin, bony face was frantic.

"But your promise?"

"What promise?"

"To her . . ."

"That woman, you mean? What about her? What have I to do with her?"

"Oh, nothing, of course. Only you told me . . ."

"Told you! Well, what if I did? You shouldn't pay so much attention to the tales people tell you. And I don't see what it has to do with you. None of your business, anyway, is it?"

"No, of course not."

"No. Then why have you come here? Why are you running after me?"

The stranger did not answer. Neither said anything for a while, nor did they look at each other.

Then Tobias spoke again: "Perhaps I did have some idea of being a pilgrim. But I've put that right out of my mind; I'm not giving it another thought. It's not for me. For I don't believe in anything, and I hold nothing sacred, so far as I know. So how could I ever be a pilgrim? How could I journey to places that they call holy, when they're not so to me? To be a pilgrim one must have something to make pilgrimage to. And I haven't."

"I understand. And you're quite right. But you said you were going for someone else's sake."

"Why should I? Who could make me? Can't a man decide for himself? I do! No one has any power over me, neither she nor . . . ! Over *you* that crucified man may have some power; he must have, by the look of you. But over me, no! What have I to do with him? And his wounds! They disgust me! *I* kneel to them! *I!* Do you imagine he could make me do that? I kneel to nothing, *nothing;* I never have . . . !

So heated was he that he hardly knew what he was doing, and his sinewy, hairy hands clenched as if to defend himself—but against whom? His eyes were frenzied.

At his feet the dog began to whimper, perhaps because of the loud and violent speech, and gazed up at him with moist, sorrowful, even reproachful eyes. At the sound of the whimper the man looked down; and suddenly, in a paroxysm of madness, he kicked the animal, sending it flying through the air. It was very sudden; it happened in an instant.

The next moment he stood as if paralysed by his own act; he could not conceive of it—could not grasp what he had done. He just stood there, his arms hanging limply at his sides.

Then he darted to the little body. He had kicked it terribly, and on the head, at which he must unconsciously have aimed, because it was from there that the look had come. The skull of the dog was cracked; blood was running from the ear and from the gaping jaws, between the small white teeth laid bare by the painfully drawn-up lip that still quivered. One eye had been forced out and was hanging, bloody and dirtied, on the thin, drab-yellow neck.

Tobias stared horrorstruck at the shattered carcase. Gasping he bent over it, knelt beside it and felt it, as if to make sure that the dog was dead, though the fact was evident. No sign of life was to be seen, no breathing, not the least movement of the ribs—nothing. And the lip had ceased quivering. There was a twitch or two of one hind leg; then it lay perfectly still. Yet Tobias stayed by it, as if to help. He couldn't have known what he was doing, and there was indeed nothing to be done.

At last he stood up, with a glance at the stranger: a despairing glance which showed how distraught he was. But he said nothing. Nor did the other, but he too was deeply affected. They both stood in silence, and only the rippling of the brook could be heard.

They stood thus for a long time, unable to make any move.

At last Tobias dragged the body of the dog in amongst the bushes on the slope and covered it with a few sprays of broom. Then they went slowly away.

When they reached the inn they found it empty. No one was in sight. All the pilgrims had gone; the gentry had left too, in their carriages; the big house stood as if deserted, with the door wide open and the wind sweeping through.

Tobias went and lay down at full length on a bench. He lay there motionless, staring into space. The stranger sat down at a little distance. They didn't speak.

After quite a long time Elizabeth entered the draughty room and saw them. She was surprised to find Tobias still there, for she knew that he had intended to make pilgrimage to the Holy Land, and thought he had gone with the others. She began talking to him about this and asking him questions, but he didn't answer. Not even she could get him to say anything or make any reply, and she went away.

But when he had been lying like that for some hours—the sun had passed the zenith and was now shining in at the west windows—he rose up from the bench, seemingly quite composed, and began to arrange his pack. As it was a very simple, modest pack, he soon finished with it, and slinging it over his shoulder he walked out.

The stranger followed him. He could not leave him alone in that queer state; he reproached himself bitterly, and felt more responsible for this man with the fierce eyes than he had ever felt for anyone before. And the incident at the brook had upset him, shaken him; it had opened as it were a gulf within him. He could not explain it, but that was how it felt. He perceived that he must go with the man—that he was bound to him in some inexplicable way and could not be parted from him. And if now for some strange reason the man was beginning his pilgrimage—as was plainly his intention—because he had kicked a dog to death, then he too must go. They belonged together.

Nor did Tobias appear to object to him as a companion; it rather seemed as if after what happened he did not want the stranger to forsake him and leave him alone with his memory. He may have felt also that now, since that unaccountable incident, they had something in common, though he could not divine why the stranger should be so deeply moved by it. But that not even the stranger himself understood as yet.

As if it were the most natural thing in the world they left the inn and started their wayfaring together.

But someone called after them, and when they turned they saw Diana hurrying towards them. She was still there, then. And Tobias, who had not once seen her that day, could not conceal his surprise that she should not have gone with her own party, the party to which she belonged. But when she began to speak of going with him instead, he firmly refused. This both angered and distressed her; at once she reproached and reviled him bitterly, at the next she begged and implored to be allowed to come.

"But you don't want to go on pilgrimage," he said.

"No, I don't. Not at all. But I want to be with you!"

This had no effect on him. But when she accused him of cruelty to her: when she told him how monstrous it was to throw her into the arms of those worthless people and force her to continue her life with them, he began to hestitate.

"And you fancy yourself a Christian!" she flung at him at last, her eyes full of tears.

He saw then that she was right: that he must allow her to come with them.

They waited while she hastily made ready, and then at last they set off.

The sun was still shining, but was now far enough to the west to make it evident that it was too late to begin the climb to the pass that day. But Tobias, who still seemed quite abstracted, never gave it a thought, and the others knew nothing about it. The sky was perfectly cloudless, and the wind light; the weather could not have been better.

Nothing of note happened as they made their way up towards the pass, except when the woman, while walking beside Tobias, happened to blurt out, "What have you done with that nasty dog?"

The savage look she received in reply silenced her abruptly, and warned her to be careful, whatever the reason. But she was glad the poor creature wasn't with them so that she was spared the sight of it.

They had now attained a considerable height; the ground all about them was covered with snow, including the valley up which they were walking, and which was becoming narrower and wilder and ever wilder. They were nearing the pass itself. By the time they reached it, tired by the steep climb, dusk was falling and a cold wind blew in their faces, stirring up the new-fallen snow on the slopes into little eddies, harmless-looking enough to anyone who did not know what they might mean up here. They went on, still able to make out their path in spite of the drifts. But suddenly, at a point where the trail rounded a projecting shoulder of rock, an icy wind hurled itself at them, bringing with it dense, whirling snow and whipping their faces so that they could see nothing in front of them. It took them utterly unawares; they stood as if blinded, calling to each other so as not to become separated. Then they stood helpless and at a loss. But Tobias, who had been here before, knew that somewhere ahead was a log cabin which had been built for pilgrims overtaken by these sudden blizzards in the pass. Or at least he believed that it lay ahead of them, and that they had not already left it behind; though because of the absent-minded state he'd been in he could not be sure. Now at last he awoke, however, and assumed leadership. The other two were to stay where they were and he would go on and look for the cabin. But this the woman would not allow. And as they could not agree, and just stood yelling at each other in the snowstorm, she set off on her own into the darkness to find it. For the light had now gone, and one could hardly see at all. She disappeared, and for a moment Tobias did not know what to do, for he could not forsake the stranger. In the end they both set off in the direction she had taken, to search for the cabin and for the woman too, lest she should lose herself altogether in the mountain. But they found neither.

After a time she shouted from a long way off that she had found the hut; then she came back and helped them to reach it. It was built close up against the mountainside, as she had known it must be, for shelter. They got the door open, and almost collapsed inside with weariness.

It was quite a small hut built of rough, unhewn logs. So much she could feel in the darkness; and on the earth floor lay a thick carpet of what seemed to be fir-branches. The wind moaned between the logs, which yet gave protection. The cabin must have been built recently for it smelt pleasently of fresh timber. She thought it a lovely place. The adventure had had a bracing effect on her, and it had been long since she had felt so content. Very long . . .

She lay, enjoying the smell of the new timber, and the harsh, fresh feel of the fir-boughs about her. She lay smiling in the dark . . . Then she fell asleep, very weary, satisfied; almost happy.

They all slept.

They must have slept well on into the day, judging by the light outside. But where the sun was they could not see, for the blizzard still continued, and all that was visible was the snow whirling furiously through the pass. It had drifted over their little house and almost buried it. The woman, who tried to peer out through an opening, was greatly struck by this; she was glad of it and declared that it made the place less draughty. She also seemed glad that they couldn't think of going on but would have to stay there, snowed in; a thing that had never happened to her before. She unpacked a little bread and goat-cheese which she had been able to snatch before leaving the inn, and shared it out. It tasted delicious, especially as there was so little of it that no one could have too much. She liked being here, that was plain; she was really enjoying it. Her face had regained much of its freshness, and her eyes were bright and eager. She seemed delighted with everything. She was delighted too at being with Tobias again, and in this way, in this kind of existence. The only thing she didn't like was his determination to make pilgrimage to that country; his stubbornness. What business had he there? It seemed to her foolish.

"Don't you think so?" she asked the stranger.

But he didn't answer. Both men fell silent when she spoke of this.

"Are you going there too?" she asked, looking into those ancient, ancient eyes that were so alien to her—so mysterious—so unlike her own, which were alert, and earthly as a hunter's.

He still made no reply.

"Is it for the sake of that crucified man? What have you to do with him?"

When he said nothing she shrugged her shoulders.

"And Tobias! What has he to do with any of that! I just don't understand!"

Tobias was silent, yet he appeared to be reflecting upon her words and to be disturbed and oppressed by them.

Then she began talking of something else, and this was evidently a relief to him.

At last the weather seemed to be clearing; the wind at any rate dropped a little and they began wondering whether they might venture out. They tried to open the door, but it was almost impossible because of all the snow: their shoving packed it hard. Only after some time could they make it yield enough for them to squeeze their way out. After that they had almost to dig their way through the drift that had built up between cabin and road. But down there the snow was not so deep, and they could struggle forward somehow.

The wind had indeed dropped, and now they

had it at their backs. Even so they could see very little, for snow still whirled about them, and they could only guess where the track ran—where it seemed most natural for it to run. The woman had the best flair for this, and walked ahead of the others. The ground was not quite even, and sloped only gently upward. Before very long their way began to run downhill. The steeps on each side of them loomed forth as the snowfall dwindled, and down beside them on the floor of the valley they heard the faint ripple of water under its fragile crust of ice: eager, playful water which could be glimpsed here and there beneath the thinning film, and flowed in the same direction as themselves.

The snow stopped falling, and the air about them cleared. At the same time the pass widened, and all at once, far below them, they beheld a broad valley opening out in radiant sunshine. It lay there like the unexpected, welcoming gateway to a joyous land, hardly to be believed in. Yet it seemed real enough, with tilled ground and little villages climbing up hills that were no longer so inordinately high. A land seemingly created for happiness and perpetual sunshine.

The woman was entranced, and for a long time she walked in silence—an unusual thing for her—just gazing at it, with unaccustomed yearning in her eyes. It was like looking into another world—a world altogether different. But how far away it seemed, despite the clarity with which every detail of it stood out. This was really something worth longing for . . .

Where they stood the land was still wild, and although the valley had widened, the slopes continued steep on either side, with moraine and fallen boulders, and low scrub where there was soil enough for it to grow. The road ran at some height along the mountainside, and from below came the sound of the little torrent, now quite free of ice. All snow had gone too, and gentle breezes came to meet them from the friendly land below. They walked easily, almost effortlessly, in the glorious air.

Suddenly they saw, some way in front of them, a large travelling-carriage which had overturned down the steep slope and been brought up short by a couple of boulders half-way to the bottom. They hurried down to it, gravel and pebbles sliding under their feet. The fore-part of it was smashed, and between the snapped shafts the horses lay dead, with their legs broken; they had been terribly wounded by their fall and were caked with clotted blood. No one was to be seen and all was quiet, which was not to be wondered at; yet in a way the effect of it was strange in contrast to the recent violence. The carriage had been abandoned, and left just as it was by those who witnessed its destruction.

But inside the half-covered vehicle they discovered the nobleman with the grand name, lying on his back with his throat cut. There he still sat, in his fine carriage, though leaning back now, and lifeless. The money chest was no longer there, nor were any of the many servants and lacqueys who had waited upon him and divined his wishes before he uttered them. Not one of them was left; he was quite alone.

The woman thought she understood what had happened; she was almost certain of it. When they were attacked, all the servants had fled, lashing their horses for their very lives; they had no wish to sacrifice their own skins for the man they had always fawned upon as if they lived only for him. And the bandits, when they had cut his throat and seized the chest which he had been so concerned about and dared not let out of his sight, drove the horses over the brink with the carriage, to make it seem like an accident; though the cut throat rendered that somewhat improbable. But such men were never particular as to detail.

This was how she accounted for it, and no doubt she was right.

"And so that money-chest never reached Jerusalem," she ended. "Didn't I tell you so?"

They stood and looked at the annihilation of recent greatness. There was now nothing left but wreckage and death. Tobias went between the two boulders to examine one of the horses, which had been stuck fast there and which he fancied showed some sign of life; for if this were so it must be helped out of its agony. But he was mistaken: there was no life there.

But the woman looked over the wild valley to the other side of the falls, unconsciously observing everything with her keen eyes. Suddenly she beheld an arrow speeding through the clear mountain air, loosed from somewhere on the opposite side; probably from among the thickets that grew there. It was aimed at them—and the next instant she saw that it was intended for Tobias; he was the target. She cried out, but Tobias, who was facing the other way, did not grasp what was happening, and in any case could not have moved quickly enough, being almost clamped between the rocks. Like lightning she darted over and threw herself in front of him, just as the arrow came.

She heard the sharp whine of it, and felt a hardly noticeable stab at her breast; it didn't hurt at all. With a painful little smile she shrank and put her hand to her heart. Then she sank to the ground.

It was all very quick. The stranger first saw what had happened, and hurried up. And when Tobias turned he was amazed to find her bleeding there on the ground with an arrow in her breast. He threw himself down and drew it out. She groaned and looked at him in reproach, for evidently that hurt very much. But to be struck by an arrow did not hurt.

He looked wildly about the landscape as if to discover whence the arrow had come, and why. But all was quiet and still. No marksman was to be seen, nothing moved either here or on the opposite side; indeed nothing had moved at any time. An arrow had flown: that was all. That was the strange thing. Where from? From whom?

Distraught, he bent over the woman who had saved his life, given her life for his. When in the utmost agitation he told her this, she just smiled at him: a pale smile. For she had turned very white, and this made her beautiful—as beautiful as she had once been, so long ago. Everything about her was pure and lovely again; she was unravaged, undeformed by anything that did not belong to her—could not really belong to her. There was nothing left of it.

She stroked his thin, bearded cheek, and said quite softly in her dark voice, "I hope you reach the land you long for."

His hand was on her hair, which lay ruffled and

thick and red about her pale face. But he could not utter a word.

Then she whispered, much more faintly than before, for her strength was gone, "Call me Diana . . . once . . . more . . ."

He bent over her and looked into her eyes, which he had not done for a long time. Why hadn't he? Why not . . . ?

"Diana . . . Diana . . . goddess of the chase . . ."

She smiled almost happily, and by that he knew that she had heard him. Then she was dead. But she was smiling a little, still.

ON A SOUTHERN SLOPE a little further down the valley grew an old oak. There they buried her, that she might rest beneath her own tree, Diana's tree. Tobias carried her there in his arms, not wanting her to lie in the gorge where she had been killed, and where so much that was horrible had happened. The oak had unusually dark foliage, for it was an evergreen oak, and thus indeed was Diana's tree. Its immemorial greenery distinguished it from everything else up here—from all that surrounded it.

Afterwards they sat and talked beside the grave. Tobias was quite broken, and full of self-reproach, because he knew he was to blame for her death and because he had so greatly wronged her; he had not taken proper care of her, or considered her, or remembered what she really was. He had much to upbraid himself with now.

To his surprise the stranger was more doubtful of his guilt. Certainly she had sacrificed herself; she had hurried forward and protected him with her own body; yet he was not altogether convinced that this was the reason for her death.

"What do you mean? I don't understand you."

"I mean, is it so certain that the arrow was intended for you?"

"Who else? It was I he was after, because I'd taken her from him—or so he thought. That's clear enough, and easy to understand."

"But you found no trace of anyone when you were over on the other side—nothing to show that anyone had been here."

"No, that's true. And it was very odd, I must own."

"Why should any of them have stayed behind after the attack? And why should he wait for you just here?"

"No, you're right. But who can it have been?"

"It's not easy to say. I don't know. But it's not impossible that the arrow might have been intended for her."

"For her? Her? But it was aimed at me; you saw that yourself."

"Yes. It would have to be. If it had been aimed at her she wouldn't have had the chance of dying for you. And that was what she had to do."

"What do you mean . . . ?"

"I mean nothing. I'm just saying that I don't know. That I can't find any real explanation. And perhaps there isn't one. That's often so."

"But you don't surely believe that she wanted to die?"

"No. I believe that the arrow wanted her to die. And wanted her death to be a happy one. And it was. Wasn't it?"

To himself he thought, What happiness to be able to die. That is the land for which a man must really yearn: the land of death, the holy land . . .

They sat silent for a time.

Then they rose and continued on their journey.

When they came down to cultivation, dusk was already falling. On the hillside lay a village or perhaps a small city; at any rate it was encircled by a wall. It was a cluster of houses that clung to the mountain and to each other, all alike, with white, almost windowless walls and pale yellow roofs. It shone in the evening sunshine. They decided to spend the night there.

There was a poor inn, which they entered. As they sat at their simple meal they learned that the company of pilgrims had passed through the day before, but without halting, and by now must have travelled a long way through the country. On hearing this, Tobias would have preferred to leave again at once, but it was impossible, for night had come and they were too tired. He slept uneasily, tossing to and fro. And in the morning, as he was going to pay, he was greatly agitated and his hand shook as he held out the money; the stranger understood why, but feigned not to notice.

When they had gone some way the man began to speak of it himself.

She had been perfectly right in saying that he had come by the money for his pilgrimage in a dishonest way. He was travelling on ill-gotten gains; he would be paying his passage to the Holy Land with stolen money, if ever he reached even the port. So now he wanted to throw it away, be rid of it; it was sin-money, won by crime; there was even blood upon it. Yet if he did this he would never reach his goal, never cross the sea, never come to the Holy Land for which he so longed. That was his predicament.

He brooded upon it, for it seemed to him to demonstrate his baseness, the dubiousness of his enterprise and of himself. He was in agony when he thought of it.

"Am I a real pilgrim? Am I?" he exclaimed distractedly.

He sat down at the roadside with his head in

his hands. His bony, bearded face was emaciated; there was now no question of haste; he just sat there, staring down at the dust of the road.

The stranger tried to help him by listening to him: the only help he could give. He listened to his doubts, his uncertainties, his indecision. Yes, he was indeed uncertain about everything.

"Tell me what it is I long for! I don't understand."

Yet he was troubled, pursued by whatever it was that he did not understand; it gave him no peace. And all at once he stood up and they resumed their wayfaring. He was eager to get on; his very indecision seemed to be spurring him on. Or else it was that with this eagerness he strove to deaden the doubts within him.

Their journey was delayed several times in this way, and they did not get on as fast as they ought. And at every halting-place, at every inn, they learned that the company of pilgrims had passed by some time before.

But at last one day they saw the sea below them, vast and open, and in the bay the little town with its pilgrims' harbour, ringed by high mountains:

the view that had filled so many wayfarers with joy and infinite longing.

The place was still a long way off, but they hoped to reach it by evening. Tobias grew much excited and wanted to hurry on as fast as they could. As he walked he looked continually out over the great waters: he had never seen the sea before, and was enthralled by it. It was dark and choppy; far out there were white horses. The wind blew off the land.

The way down took longer than they had expected, for the road wound along the mountainsides and only gradually descended towards the sea. The day was near its end and when at last they reached the town it was almost dark. They only just entered the city gate before it was closed for the night.

They knew of a monastery here where pilgrims lodged while awaiting a passage. It was not far from the harbour, and they asked their way to it.

Outside the gate a little flame was burning before an image of the Madonna. They knocked, and a brother came out. When they enquired about the pilgrim-ship that was soon to sail for the Holy Land they learned that it had left port that day, not long after noon, for the wind had been favourable and all the companies of pilgrims from different places had arrived here. No other ship was to leave, for soon the autumn gales would begin, and during the winter half of the year there were no sailings.

Tobias, hearing this, was utterly cast down. His lips quivered and he could scarcely utter a word; barely a word of thanks to the brother for his information—for the sentence he had passed upon him unawares.

For a sentence it was. A fearful sentence upon him, and an unmistakable sign. Just as he arrived at the sea—at the pilgrims' port—the vessel carrying the real, the true pilgrims had sailed, spreading her canvas for the voyage over the unknown waters to the land that they, but not he, would see.

Thus it was. Thus it had to be.

Thus it was, and thus it had to be . . . He repeated the words to himself and they filled him with a despair such as he had never felt before, or ever dreamt he could feel. What he had lost, what he was not to attain, what he had not been chosen to experience, stood forth to him as the only goal—the only thing worth living for—living and dying for. To lose it was to lose his soul and virtually to exist no longer, either here in time or in eternity; to lose all hope. He stared out into the night, and his eyes were wild with desolation and hopelessness and with a glow that would not die, though it ought to have died now and for ever.

The other two noticed nothing, for it was dark, and the light of the little flame by the Madonna did not reach him. Suddenly, as they were standing there, he vanished from them into the darkness. He was engulfed by it, and was no more beside them. The brother looked in surprise at the stranger, who stammered that he didn't understand, and that he must go and look for him. The monk nodded assent, and they parted.

Nowhere in the neighbouring alleyways did he find him. He searched further and further, until he had covered the greater part of the little town, but the man was nowhere to be found. He couldn't understand where he had gone. He asked one or two passers-by if they had seen him, but they had not.

At last it struck him that perhaps he should go down to the harbour, although there was really no sense in that. What had the vanished man to do there, and at this time of night?

The harbour lay dark and deserted. From away in the night came the muffled, menacing boom of open water: high seas must be running, though there was little sign of them in here. It was a well-sheltered harbour fashioned by nature herself; the very quay seemed almost a natural formation which had merely been improved here and there. There was no one about so far as he could see at first, and not a single ship; only a few fishing-craft drawn up on the shore. But alongside the very end of the quay, right against the cliff, lay a vessel that was just hoisting sail. The canvas flapped and slapped as it was spread; it was this that told him that something was going on there, and he walked towards the sound.

A lantern hung from the yard, and on the quay beneath it stood a few men apparently in animated conversation. On coming nearer he found to his surprise and bewilderment that one of them was Tobias. He didn't see him at first, for he stood in the middle, surrounded by the rest. There were three men, whose faces were not the kind to inspire confidence; they were questionable characters. In fact they looked thorough-going scoundrels. How had Tobias fallen in with them?

He went still nearer, though not close enough to be seen, and was able to hear what they were saying.

The men were evidently telling Tobias that they were bound for the Holy Land in their yawl and that he might sail with them if he paid them well. There was much talk of payment; he could hear that. No doubt they were trying to discover how much he had, so as to adjust their price accordingly. Tobias was finding it difficult to understand them, but the important part was easy to grasp. They vowed that they really were bound for the Holy Land and that they wanted a great deal of money. Tobias was excited, and his lean face looked almost feverish in the flickering light of the lantern.

At last he took out his money—all of it, without any doubt—and his hand shook as he held it out to the men. They snatched it and counted it greedily, and were plainly astonished at the amount; all the same they told him that it was really too little, but that he might come anyway.

They seemed suddenly in a great hurry, and began whispering to one another to make haste. The final preparations for sailing were rapidly made and Tobias was almost pushed abroad. It really looked as if for some reason the boat was compelled to leave port. What shady business these men were about it was hard to say, but there was reason enough to think that all was not as it should have been. The vessel herself looked suspect as she lay rocking at her moorings, with the wind tearing impatiently at her dirty sail. She was battered and ill-cared-for, and matched the riff-raff who sailed her.

"The Holy Land!" laughed the fellow as he threw the hawser aboard and swung himself over the rail. He said something to another of the crew, of just as ruffianly an aspect, and they stood laughing raucously together. Tobias was not to be seen.

The vessel glided from the quay, and her sail filled at once. The wind must have risen considerably, and would be blowing hard out at sea. The yawl left the harbour at a fair speed and vanished further and further into the night. The stranger stood watching her, following her on her way into the unknown. At last she could be seen no longer, and all was darkness.

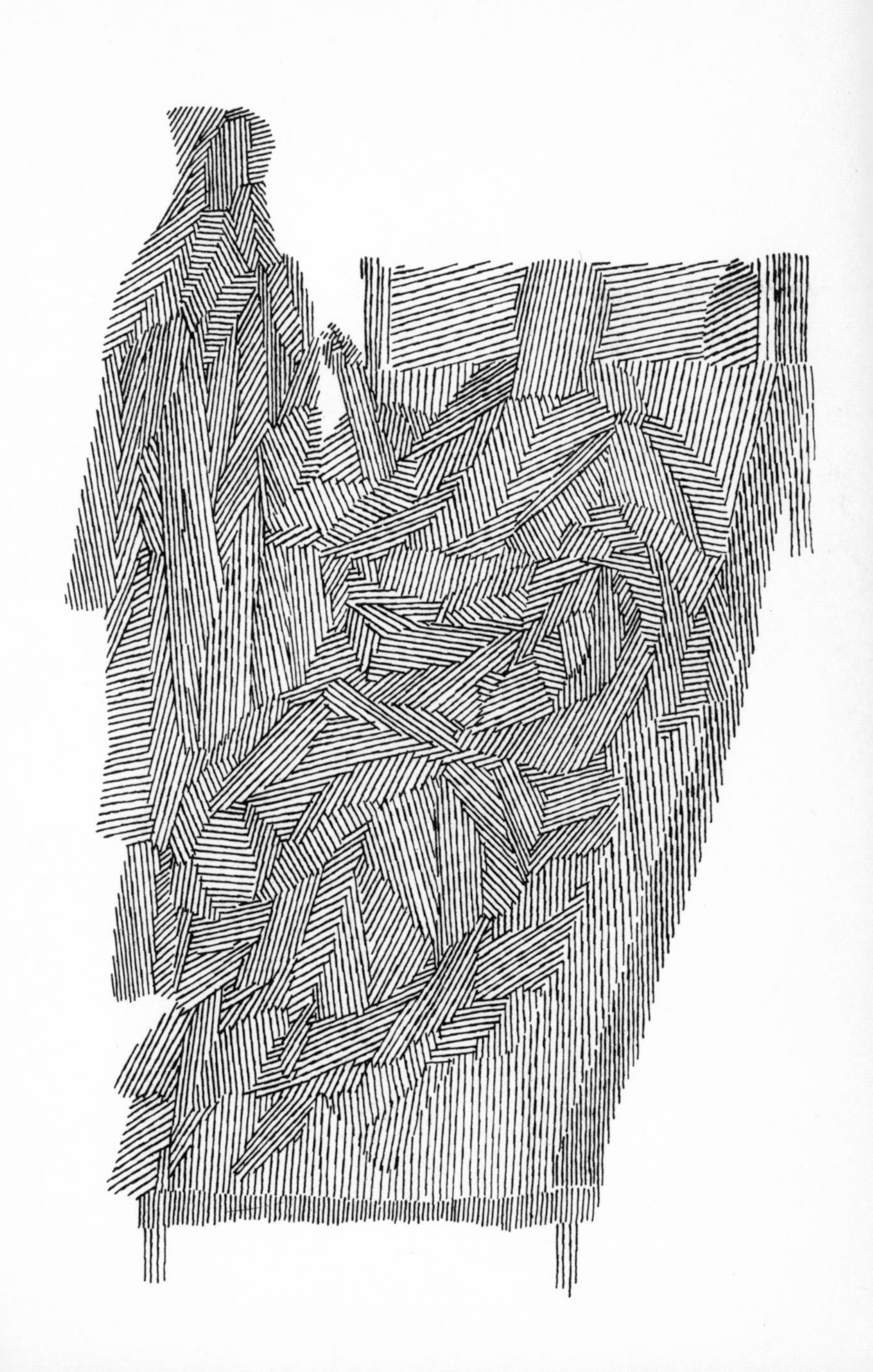

"WHY DO YOU persecute me? Why do you never leave me in peace? Why do you never forsake me?

"What have I done to you that you should be revenged, that you should always be thinking of your vengeance? What did I do? I forbade you to lean your head against my house. That's all. Isn't it?

"How many others have done the same? But me

you will not forgive—me you will not forget. Although it was so long ago. Since then many have denied you the same thing, so many that you can't remember them. But me you remember, me you never forget. And I don't forget you.

"Why do you force me to think of you continually? To think of how you came along the street, dragging your cross? What was so strange about that? I lived in that street, and I'd seen the same thing countless times, ever since I was a child. Why then should I have paid so much attention that time —so much attention to you? If a man lives in a street where men keep coming with their crosses, how is he to notice one day that one of them is god's son? How can you expect it? You expect too much. You're too unmerciful to me, in your demands on me.

"You think you're the only one to endure your fate, your suffering, your crucifixion. But you know very well you're not. You're only one among many, in an endless procession. All mankind is crucified, like you; man himself is crucified; you're just the one they look up to when they think of their fate and their suffering, and of how they are victims of sacrifice; you're the one whom therefore they call the Son of Man. I understand this; I discovered it at last: man lies forsaken on his bed of torment in a desolate world, sacrificed and forsaken, stretched out upon a little straw, marked by the same wounds as yourself. Suffering and sacrifice are spread over the whole earth and throughout all time, though only you are called the Crucified—only you among all those who have been so; when one thinks of pain and anguish and injustice one thinks of you. As if there were no other pain than yours, no other injustice than that committed against you.

"But who was it who made them crucify you, who consigned you to suffering and death? Who sacrificed you—you whom he called his own son, who made you believe you were so? Who demanded this sacrifice, which he demanded of so many others—the sacrifice above every sacrifice, the sacrifice that was never to be forgotten, the sacrifice of the chosen one himself? Who offered up the Son of Man?

"You should know; you should know what he's like—you who persist in calling him your father, though he has never cared about you, never shown that he loves you; though he let you hang there when you cried out to him in your deepest despair: 'Why have you forsaken me?' Have you forgotten this? Have you forgotten how he forsook you?

"He sacrifices men! He demands continual sacrifice—human sacrifice, crucifixions! That's what he's like, if you would only listen to me. I know—I who have dragged my curse with me through the ages, dragged it as you dragged your cross, only much further than you. My curse as the enemy of god, the repudiator, the blasphemer, the rebel against god. For it was he who cursed me, not you. I know that: I've come to understand that at last. You just uttered what he prompted you to say. His was the power and the vengeance. What power had you! You yourself had been handed over, sacrificed, forsaken. Now I understand: you were my brother. He who pronounced the curse on me was my own brother, himself an unhappy, accursed man.

"Now I understand it all. For now I have torn down the veil of the holy of holies and seen who he is. Now at last he has lost his power over me. At last I have overcome him—at last I have vanquished god!

"I have lifted the curse from my own shoulders. I have delivered myself from my destiny and mastered it. Not with your help or anyone else's, but by my own strength. I have saved myself. I have conquered. I have conquered god.

"That is why I lie here and feel death approaching: kind, merciful death, which I have yearned for for so long—which was not to be vouchsafed me.

"Now I feel it coming to me in its great mercy; life's sister, who would have nothing to do with me, is coming—stroking my brow with her cool hand, which alone can console and give peace. It is long since anyone caressed me. But no hand have I longed for as I have longed for yours. Now I know you won't leave me; that you will stay until you take me with you to your kingdom; till you lead me into your holy land.

"How long have I lain in this house of stillness? How long is it since I came here, since that night of storm when the pilgrim who was no real pilgrim fled into the night—into the unknown—to what? How long since I lay listening to the gale out at sea, as it blew ever more fiercely? Blew, it may be, to his destruction? Or did he arrive? Arrive where?

"What he longed for I don't know, but it must have been something of the utmost importance. Even if he perished in the storm, even if the rabble on that boat cheated him and perhaps carried him off to some quite other place, what he longed for must nevertheless have been of the utmost importance. That he made me understand. Something so important that it were better to lose one's life rather than one's faith in that thing.

"That it is so, even I, the enemy of god, the blasphemer and repudiator, must acknowledge. And I acknowledge it readily.

"Beyond the gods, beyond all that falsifies and coarsens the world of holiness, beyond all lies and distortion, all twisted divinities and all the abortions of human imagination, there must be something stupendous which is inaccessible to us. Which, by our very failure to capture it, demonstrates how inaccessible it is. Beyond all the sacred clutter the holy thing itself must exist. That I believe, of that I am certain.

"God is nothing to me. Indeed he is hateful to me, because he deceives me about this very thing, and hides it from me. Because, believing that we long for him, he withholds what we do long for. Because he keeps us from it.

"Yes, god is what divides us from the divine. Hinders us from drinking at the spring itself. To god I do not kneel—no, and I never will. But I would gladly lie down at the spring to drink from it—to quench my thirst, my burning thirst for what I cannot conceive of, but which I know exists. At the spring I would gladly kneel.

"And perhaps that is what I'm doing now. Now that the battle is over at last and I may die. Now that at last I have won peace.

"I don't know what it hides in its dark depths. If I did I might well be terrified. But I desire to drink from it. It may be those very depths that can assuage my burning thirst."

He lay looking out at the little bare white room, which to his weary eyes had no determined limits, but was merely a cleanliness and lightness in which he rested. Outside, the sea no longer murmured as it had been doing all the time; or perhaps he could no longer hear it? Perhaps all earthly sounds, all earthly murmurings were gone from him—perhaps he could no longer hear such things? He must be in a kind of swoon—a swoon of light.

Someone opened the door cautiously and came in. He couldn't move his head, or even see plainly any longer, but he knew that it must be the little lay-brother who regularly looked in to make sure that he lacked for nothing. It must be he, though he could no longer see him.

He would very gladly have beheld that wrinkled little face with its ever-friendly smile, but although the newcomer approached the bed, he could not discern it. It was sad that he couldn't see it—that he would never see it again. Never again would he behold a human face. Strange that he should regret this—he who during his life-time had had no particular love for his fellow-men.

There was something odd about this little brother, who had taken care of him and tended him so lovingly throughout. He seemed somehow familiar, as if one had met him before; he had felt that from the beginning, but could not make out where or when. It was probably imagination. But as he watched him walking about this cell on his bare feet, which were quite black underneath because he always walked barefoot, there seemed something familiar about the sight: it was something that he remembered. But he could never make out why.

The little man was not a monk, just a serving brother who tended the sick, as he was now tending the stranger. He was the humblest of men and seemed perfect in goodness, naturally good, and it was really an infinite wonder that such a one as he should exist at all. The man about to die could not but be thankful that the last human being he was to meet should be this one.

He now felt him straightening the pillow. It was a delight to know that he was there. But he saw him merely as something dark; as a shadow beside him.

All at once the room was filled with radiant light. It was extraordinary. And it happened suddenly, as by a miracle.

"What's this light—this glorious light I can see?" he whispered faintly, so faintly that the little lay-brother could hardly catch it. But he understood what the dying man must be asking, for the sun had broken through the clouds and was now shining straight into the room through the little window in the south wall that faced the sea.

He bent down and explained that the clouds had dispersed and that the sun was shining straight in upon him. For he wanted to say no more than the truth, and to state the facts as they were. And the dying man appeared content with this simple explanation of something that had filled him with great wonder. He shut his eyes, but still felt the light upon them: that it was there, that it *was*.

And with this light—the light so familiar to earth—upon him, he left the world.

For a long time the little lay-brother stood looking at the dead man—at his remarkable face, which now radiated so perfect a tranquility. It had not done so when he came here that stormy night. What had so changed him?

Who could he be, this stranger, this singular guest? He didn't know. No one in the monastery knew. Was he really a pilgrim? Was he even Christian? No one knew.

But his peace was great. That one could see.

ABOUT THE AUTHOR

PÄR LAGERKVIST, Swedish Nobel Prize winner, uses materials of the past to express modern ideas. For half a century he has developed as a creative artist, and his work includes more than thirty-five volumes of fiction, drama, poems and essays. Though his early reputation was based on the philosophy contained in his plays, wide translation of his other writings has won him many devotees in both hemispheres.

When Americans were introduced to *Barabbas,* a haunting tale of Calvary, in 1951, a critic said: "He has only to indicate, to draw a sharp and poignant line, and his collaborator, the twentieth-century reader, can fill in his own background." This book has been filmed recently in Rome by Dino De Laurentiis, to be released through Columbia Pictures in the spring. Two other novels, *The Dwarf* and *The Sibyl,* have been published in this country, as well as *The Eternal Smile,* a collection of short stories.

Apart from extended visits to Denmark, France and Italy, Lagerkvist has lived chiefly in Sweden, where he was educated at the University of Upsala. In 1940 he was elected one of the eighteen "immortals" of the Swedish Academy.